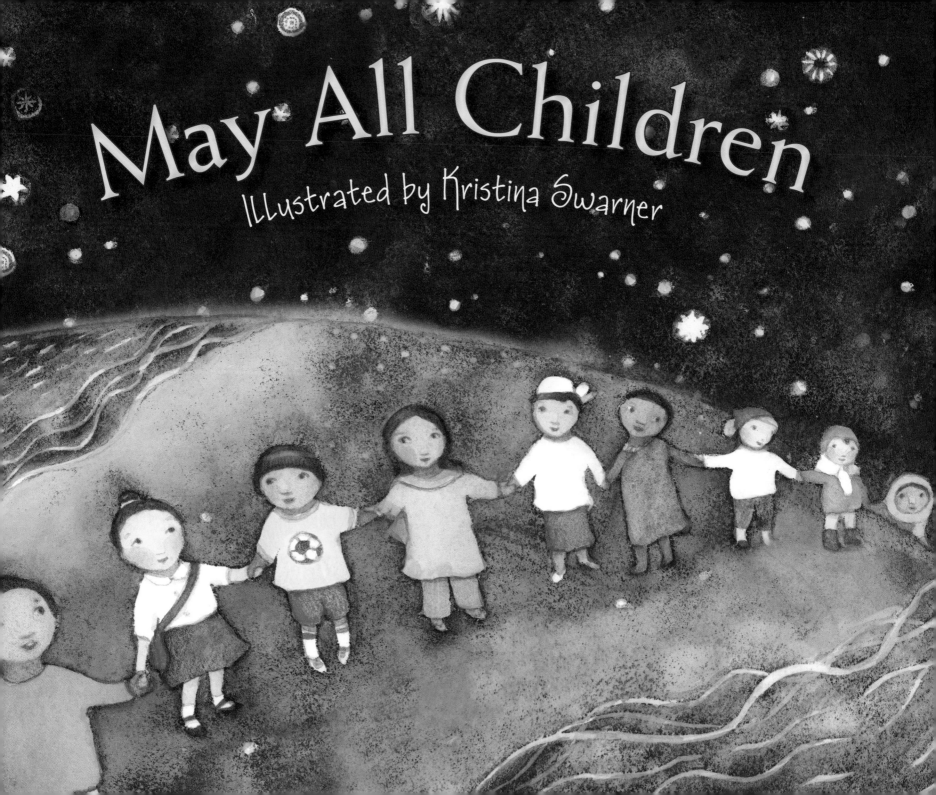

May All Children

Illustrated by Kristina Swarner

ISBN 978-0-9855719-6-2
Printed in Mexico on FSC® paper
from well-managed forests

Music Together LLC
66 Witherspoon Street
Princeton NJ 08542
www.musictogether.com
(800) 728-2692

MUSIC TOGETHER®

May All Children

Welcome

Since 1987, Music Together has been bringing the Joy of Family Music® to young children and their families. This Singalong Storybook offers a new way to enjoy one of our best-loved Music Together songs. We invite you to sing it, read it, and use it as a starting point for conversation and imaginative play with your child.

Using the Book

If you're a Music Together family, you might start singing as soon as you turn the pages. But even if you've never attended one of our classes, you and your child can have hours of fun and learning with this Singalong Storybook. Read the story and enjoy the illustrations with your child, and then try some of the suggested activities that follow. The book can also help inspire artwork or enhance pre-literacy skills. You can even invent your own variations of the story or involve the whole family in some musical dramatic play.

Using the Recording Of course, you can also get a recording of the song to enhance your enjoyment of the book. See page 31 for ways to get the Singalong Storybook songs and see the video "Using Your Singalong Storybook Musically." Or, if you play an instrument such as piano or guitar, you'll find it easy to pick out the song using the music page at the end of the book.

May,
    may all,
        may all children,

7

May all people everywhere
hear this prayer.

9

May,
    may all,
        may all children,

May all people everywhere
live in peace,

13

14

Sweet peace.

Peaceful minds,

Peaceful hearts,

Peace on earth.

Sweet . . .

peace

on

earth.

Activities

Call-and-Response

Parts of this song can be sung call-and-response style.
Try this with your child or another adult:

Parent:	May	**Child:**	May
Parent:	May all	**Child:**	May all
Parent:	May all children	**Child:**	May all children

Together: May all people everywhere hear this prayer…

Discussion

Talk to your child about what it means to have a peaceful
mind or a peaceful heart. What does that feel like?
Even children as young as three may be able to verbalize
what being "peaceful" means to them, and what situations
or activities help make them feel this way.

Lullaby

Snuggle with your child and sing this song at bedtime. A lullaby has a unique power to bond and soothe. Also, when your child is upset, singing this song together can help shift the mood.

Musical Arrangements

Several arrangements of "May all Children" are available on the Music Together website, where you can also see a log of the many schools, church groups, and choruses that have performed it in different settings around the world. If you are interested in singing the song in your own school or church, downloads of the music notation are free, and all donated royalties go directly to UNICEF. It is our hope that those who work with children or music in any way will use this song and sing out its wish for the world.

May All Children

K. Guilmartin

Gently

May, may all, may all chil-dren,___ May all

peo-ple ev-'ry - where hear this prayer.___ May, may

all, may all chil-dren,___ May all peo-ple ev-'ry -

where live in peace,___ Sweet_____

peace.___ Peace-ful minds, peace-ful hearts, peace on

earth.___ Sweet_____ peace on earth.

About the Song

This song was written by Kenneth K. Guilmartin in 1986 for the Montclair Cooperative School, where Ken was developing what was to become Music Together. Originally titled "Solstice Song," it was written for the school's celebration of the fortieth anniversary of UNICEF. Ken later rearranged and retitled the song in memory of September 11, 2001.

The message of the song is not offered in any political or religious context. Rather, its simple, heartfelt wish for peace on earth arises from a universal longing shared across the world.

About Music Together®

Music Together classes offer a wide range of activities that are designed to be engaging and enjoyable for children from birth through age seven. By presenting a rich tonal and rhythmic mix as well as a variety of musical styles, Music Together provides children with a depth of experience that stimulates and supports their growing music skills and understanding.

Developed by Founder/Director Kenneth K. Guilmartin and his coauthor, Director of Research Lili M. Levinowitz, Ph.D., Music Together is built on the idea that all children are musical, that their parents and caregivers are a vital part of their music learning, and that their natural music abilities will flower and flourish when they are provided with a sufficiently rich learning environment.

And it's fun! Our proven methods not only help children learn to embrace and express their natural musicality—they often help their grateful grownups recapture a love of music, too. In Music Together classes all over the world, children and their families learn that music can happen anywhere, every day, at any time of the day—and they learn they can make it themselves.

Known worldwide for our mixed-age family classes, we have also adapted our curriculum to suit the needs of infants, older children, and children in school settings such as preschools, kindergartens, and early elementary grades. Visit www.musictogether.com to see video clips of Music Together classes; read about the research behind the program; purchase instruments, CDs, and books; and find a class near you. Keep singing!

Getting the Music

"May All Children" has been sung in Music Together classes around the world. At www.musictogether.com/storybooks you can listen to the song free. You can also find it on the award-winning Music Together CDs **Family Favorites**® and **Lullabies**. CDs and downloads are available from Music Together, iTunes, and Amazon. To get the most out of your storybook, see the video "Using Your Singalong Storybook Musically" on our website.

These CDs include some of the most-loved Music Together songs, along with 32-page booklets with many family activities to enjoy. Our award-winning **Family Favorites**® **Songbook for Teachers** features techniques and activities to suit a variety of classroom settings.

Come visit us at **www.musictogether.com**.

Music Together LLC

Kenneth K. Guilmartin, Founder/Director

Catherine Judd Hirsch, Director of Publishing and Marketing

Marcel Chouteau, Manager of Production and Distribution

Jill Bronson, Manager of Retail and Market Research

Susan Pujdak Hoffman, Senior Editor

Developed by Q2A/Bill Smith, New York, NY

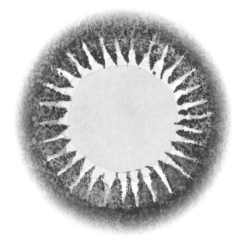